C
BLU!

# FOLK MUSIC

Here is the truth that so many in the Folk Music world wanted to hide.

The club and festival organisers, singers, dancers, instrumentalists, posers, con-men, and peoples' heroes who wear their underpants outside their tights whilst strumming an out-of-tune guitar, are now exposed for what they are. You will soon know all their secrets!

So that you can move with ease in the world of Folk Music this book deciphers every cliche. Those simply listening can now decode the true meaning of every obscure piece of jargon. Conversationalists can baffle their friends on arcane subjects such as ethnomusicology.

In succinct prose this volume describes the Folk Music Environment including the exclusive Clubs and Festivals, and unravels some baffling definitions. We learn of the subtleties of Folk Song, and the personalities of this world.

The tense moments of the performance are closely examined. What to listen for and what to say are both addressed. Instruments, their use and abuse, are all debated. Folk dancing is discussed in detail. Icons of the genre are explained, and even the flora and fauna of this strange world are explored.

Finally, to demonstrate that no stone is left unturned, the use and abuse of electronics is discussed, and the shocking ailments of this lifestyle are revealed to all.

Armed with this handy volume you can comment knowledgeably, achieve dramatically swift social acceptance, and rapidly become one of the cognoscenti.

# CONTENTS

1. The Folk Environment — 4
2. Folk Personalities — 6
3. The Folk Club — 7
4. The Folk Festival — 9
5. Folk Song — 11
6. The Performance — 12
7. Folk Instruments — 13
8. Instrumental Work — 15
9. Useful Musical Terms — 16
10. Folk Dancing — 18
11. Dance Glossary — 19
12. Traditional Characters — 21
13. Traditional Stereotypes — 22
14. Folk Geography — 24
15. Icons in the Tradition — 26
16. Traditional Pastimes — 28
17. Folk Flora and Fauna — 30
18. Folk Ailments — 31
19. Electronics for Folkies — 32

# ◆ THE FOLK ENVIRONMENT

**Folk Music:** anything acceptable in a folk club.
**Folk Song:** any song acceptable in a folk club.
**Folk Dance:** extrovert anti-social activity between consenting (& usually sweaty) adults.
**Folk Festival:** device to boost folk agency income and/or consumption of real ale.
**Folk Club:** gathering place for old, opinionated would-be musicians.

> **Traditional Ambience:** excessive alcohol.
> **Singers' Night:** competitive arena for incompetent locals.
> **Guest Night:** when antagonisms are aimed at visitors instead of locals.
> **Sing Around:** entertainment for sado-masochists.

**Culturally Significant:** not English.
**Celtic:** superficially culturally significant.
**Loud:** French or Scottish.
**Quiet:** deaf.

**Sharp:**
(1): definitive early Collector, fashionable to decry under ethnic or ecological pretext.
(2): see Traditional Tuning.

**Compact Disc:**
(1): device to bolster folk artists ego.
(2): device to boost income of folk agency.

**Field Recording:**
(1): cheap CD.
(2): tape of someone elses CD.
(3): illicit recording at a Club or Festival.

**Raffle**:
(1): main source finance of folk clubs.
(2): disposal method for unwanted tapes.

**Source:**
(1): see Songwriter.
(2): anyone, given enough Traditional Ambience.

# ◆ FOLK PERSONALITIES

**Festival Organiser:** failed club organiser.
**Folk Group:** successful imposition of the will of one musician on compliant colleagues.

**Club Organiser:** failed performer.
**Club Resident:** failed organiser.
**Club Committee:** failed residents.
**Club Secretary:** weakest failed resident.
**Collector:** provider of Ambience, owner of Walkman.

**MC:** one who could think of no excuse.
(See also: Loudest voice/ biggest head.)

**Newsletter Writer:** the one who collates all the gossip (see Raffle Ticket Seller and Barmaid)

**Raffle Ticket Seller:** either a refugee from the Inland Revenue, or the MCs last-but-one girlfriend.

**Barmaid:** the girlfriend before that.

**Singer/songwriter:** one who can't remember others' lyrics.
**Soloist:** solitary misanthrope.
**Source:** consumer of Ambience.

**Traditional Singer:** one incapable of accompanying him/herself.
**Accompanist:** one incapable of singing.
**Instrumentalist:** one who knows he can't sing.

**Audience:**
(1) singers who have not yet plucked up courage.
(2) singers who have been banned.

**Enthusiast:** buys 2 strips of raffle tickets.
**Expert:** arrives late enough to avoid paying.
**Cognoscenti:** arrives when the guest artist starts.

# ◆ THE FOLK CLUB

**Arrival:** It is traditional to arrive late, clinking glasses and rustling crisp packets. This is always taken as a sign of your enthusiasm for the genre and appreciation of those who performed before you arrived.

**Beer Breaks:** Similar to the Arrival. Do not wait outside until an artist has finished. Always show your enthusiasm by rushing in to savour every second of the performance. It is advisable to sit at the front to fully appreciate the music.

**Performance:** Artists always appreciate you showing your understanding of their work by talking to friends and discussing salient points during the performance.

**Response** (1): Always show your appreciation of a quiet song or slow air by being the first to shout "Oh Yes" in the last seconds of the performance. Never let the sound die without a response.

**Response** (2): It is unnecessary to applaud up-tempo numbers. Everyone else will already be clapping and your response will go unnoticed.

**Departure:** It is traditional to leave early in order to catch the last bus, train, dance, or partner. This is best done during (not between) numbers, to ensure that the audience believes that you are sufficiently important to have a pressing engagement elsewhere.

## ✓ *Folk Club Checklist*

Sets of raffle tickets in all colours.
Sidmouth tee shirt (you need not have been there).
Out-of-tune pitch pipe (to lend to rivals).
Electronic guitar tuner (discretely hidden).
Broken capo and plectrum (also to lend).
Empty crisp packets (see Arrival).
Walkman (see Field Recordings).
EFDSS badge (you don't have to belong, just get the badge.)

# ◆ THE FOLK FESTIVAL

**Arrival**. On arrival identify and enter the noisiest pub. Here you will always find the best Ambience. It is not necessary to leave under your own volition.

**Festival Office.** Never go to the festival office. It is rarely worth being seen there, it will be very busy, and those working there will welcome any reduction in workload..

**The Campsite.** Always erect your tent in the dark after completing the arrival as described above. The Ambience and darkness always help the erection. Do not disturb the camp-site steward, he will have had a long evening checking everyone else, and in the morning he will appreciate the artistic license you will undoubtedly demonstrate in siting your tent.

**Concerts.** Do not trouble the stewards. They are always busy and will be pleased if they do not have to check your ticket as well as every one elses.

# ✓ _Festival Checklist_

Welly boots (see Ailments).
Cagoule (to ensure sun).
Ear-plugs: see Bodhran, Hurdy-gurdy, sleep.
Greenpeace tee shirt (to ensure acid rain).
Holy jeans & Jesus sandals (for the Sunday concert).
Folding stool (to make sure you can sit at the front).
Joss sticks (you are bound to camp near the loo).
Knife (for bagpipes)
Fork (for bodhrans)
Spoons (to signal the correct rhythm to those on stage)
Screaming child (to leave in workshops)
Shades (to ensure cloud).
Tankard slung on belt (see Ambience).
Walkman (see Field Recordings).

## ◆ FOLK SONG

**Traditional:** concerns lust, cross-dressing, voyeurism & killing things.
**Self-penned:** derivative.
**Australian:** by Martyn Wyndham-Read.
**American:** by Alan Lomax or Tom Paxton.
**Ballad:** long story with background music. (See also: Sleep.)
**Bob Dylan:** written by Ewan McColl.
**Ewan McColl:** see work song.
**Folk-rock:** Ashley Hutchins' meal ticket (see Albion Band and Insomnia)
**Forebitter:** written by Cyril Tawney.
**Shanty:**
(1): written by Stan Hugill.
(2): see Repetitious, Tuneless, Noisy.
**Shapenote Music:** Janet+John do Tonic Sol-fa.
**Story:** Ballad without music.
**Work Song:** one written by a left-wing pinko commie sympathiser.
**Hunting Song:** written by a right-wing bloodthirsty fascist sympathiser.
**Wassail:** Christmas carol not about Christmas.
**West Gallery:** harmony for snobs.

# ◆ THE PERFORMANCE

**Pure Tone:** nasal.
**Traditional Tone:** cracked.
**Traditional Posture:** erect, hand around beer.
**Modern Posture:** hunched, hand around ear.
**Modern Phrasing:** breathing edited-out.
**Traditional Phrasing:** 1 breath per bar (see 5/4 time).
**Challenged In The Upper Register:**
(1): can't sing high.
(2): transvestite/gay.
**Challenged In The Lower Register:**
(1): can't sing low.
(2): lesbian.
**Syncopation:** poor timing.
**Close Harmony:** failed unison.
**Interpreted With Character:** no sense of pitch or rhythm.
**Sensitive Accompaniment:** inaudible.
**Insensitive Accompaniment:** played on the accordion.
**Modern Accompaniment:** singer inaudible.
**Emotional:** see Ambience.
**Without Emotion:** lacking in Ambience.

# ◆ FOLK INSTRUMENTS

**Accordion:** placebo for non-musicians.
**Appalachian Dulcimer:** triumph of folk carpentry over acoustics.
**Auto-harp:**
(1): small misappropriated egg-slicer.
(2): triumph of mechanics over musicality.

**Banjo:** tunable side-drum.
**Bodhran:** placebo for admitted non-musicians.
**Bombarde:** French weapon (see Common Agricultural Policy)
**Bones:** ghoulish but pocketable equivalent to the washboard.
**Bouzouki:**
(1): Anti-tank weapon.
(2): Greek liqueur.
**Fibreglass Guitar:** invention of the amplifier industry.

**Fiddle:**
(1): bad violin.
(2): device kept in knapsack for female titillation, see also Oboe & Trombone.

**Guitar:** psychological crutch for bad singers.
**Hammer Dulcimer:** large misappropriated egg-slicer.
**Hardanger Fiddle:** one with spare strings built-in.
**Hurdy-Gurdy:** deranged mechanical bumble-bee.
**Jews' or Jaws Harp:** primitive dental tool for removing plaque.

**Melodeon:** linear Concertina, has the social properties of the Accordion.
**Mouth Organ:** unsafe reed instrument.
**Concertina:** mouth organ in a leather condom.
**Pan Pipes:** wind instrument without reeds, originally made from reeds.
**Spoons:** vegetarian equivalent of Bones. (Useful for curry take-aways & mushy peas.)

**Uillean (or Union) Pipes:** deranged manual vacuum cleaner.
**Washboard:** musical equivalent of the machine-gun.
**Whistle:** tuneless perforated straw (see Tankard).

# ◆ INSTRUMENTAL PERFORMANCE

**Capo:** substitute for instrumental technique enabling guitarists to use only 3 chords.

**Tuning:**
(1): ritual in which the audience gets used to out-of-tune instruments.
(2): pause whilst singer remembers words or spins out time.
**Traditional Tuning:** out of tune.
**Modern Tuning:** guitarist uses funny chords.
**Open Tuning:** substitute for guitar technique permitting (with a capo) use of only 2 chords.

**Fiddle Styles:**
    **Mountain:** can't play on less than 2 strings.
    **Scots:** metronome attached to the elbow.
    **Irish:** changes bow direction at each end, regardless of timing.
    **English:** can't play on less than 2 strings, & changes bow on each note. Tempo controlled by length of bow & aggression of player.
    **Swedish:** duets with random timing.

# ◆ USEFUL MUSICAL TERMS

**Bar:** source of Ambience.
**Bar Line:** occurs when they change barrels.
**Bass Clef:** the key to the beer cellar.
**Bass Line:** sophisticated Bar Line.
**B flat:** term applied to most wind instruments.
**Bottom C:** late night precursor to Duet.

**Clef:** it always feels like one between the festival location and the camp site.
**Counter Melody:** when the accompanist knows the tune better than the soloist.
**Counterpoint:** when the accompanist knows a better tune than the soloist.

**Dual Tonic:** accompaniment for double gin.
**Dutch Capo:** see Duet.
**Encore:** consequence of a limited repertoire.
**Flattened Seventh:** action to form sextet.

**G-String:** unreliable cliche.
**Harmony:** random instinctive vocalisation.
**Improvisation:** poorly disguised error.

**Key Signature:** organiser's autograph on admission pass.
**Melody:** the loudest performer sings/plays it.
**Mute:** concept unknown to accordion and bodhran players.
**Pitch:** action to reduce volume of undesirable musical contribution.
**Perfect Pitch:** ability to hurl a banjo into a WC without touching the rim from a range of 5 yds.
**Quartet:** two pints (see Ambience).

**Relative Pitch**: variant of Pitch, (see Workshops and Screaming Child.)
**Repeat Bar:** location for 2nd half of Quartet.
**Score:** often follows Bottom C.
**Scotch Snap:** swift whisky consumption.
**Sextet:** see Bottom C and Duet.
**Treble Clef:** score used by a trio.
**Middle C:** another name for the Mediterranean.
**Tonic:** accompaniment for gin.
**Top C:** often associated with Country Dancing and T-Shirts.

## ◆ FOLK DANCING

**Starting.** Always join a complete set. It will save you having to start a new one. One couple will always be delighted to make space for you.

**Position.** If by chance the other dancers in the set identify you as being "top couple" immediately demur, feigning modesty, and insist that everyone else moves along one place.

**Calling.** Do not concern yourself with the caller. The other dancers will be delighted at your ability to extemporise on the dance floor.

**The Dance.** During dances speak severely to any one critical of your technique, they are only envious. Now is the time to show extravagant footwork and variations upon the set dance.

**In Between Dances.** Use the time between dances for solo demonstrations of your technique. They will enhance your reputation.

# ◆ DANCE GLOSSARY

**Barn Dance:** ceilidh (see Inverted Snobbery).

**Caller:** domineering female, shouts at dancers.
**Cajun:** repetitive foreign dance requiring one leg longer than the other.
**Ceilidh:** poser's name for a barn dance.

**Clog:**
(1): female activist exhibitionism.
(2): tap dancing for the over-40s.

**Country Dance Band:** music machine (see Accordion).

**English:** dance with random footwork.
**Irish:** footwork with enough lift to succeed in a peat bog.

**Morris:** excuse for weak-jawed men to grow beards and wield pit props.
**Ladies' Morris:** excuse for dominant women to to grow beards and wield pit props.

**Scots:** dance with mechanical footwork. Requires appropriate music (see Country Dance Band)

**Rapper:** fast dance for double-jointed men.
**Long-Sword:** fast dance for single-jointed men.

**Sword:** step dance with lethal obstructions.

**Sets:**
   **Square:** 4 couples in competition.
   **Longways**: 2 teams in competition.
   **Circular:** every man for himself.

**Chains:**
   **Ladies:** women can handle women.
   **Grand:** everybody can handle each other.

**Basket:** chance for men to manhandle women legally, or women to legally strangle men.

**Star:** revolution by over 2 dancers.
**Strip the Willow:** interactive confusion.

# ◆ PERSONALITIES OF THE TRADITION

**Bonaparte:** Irish hero.
**Childe:** inventor of the ballad.
**Jack:** tar-covered, tends to pull strings tied to naked women.
**Jock Stewart:** Scots philanthropist.
**Judy:** Liverpudlian haulier.
**Marys:** used to be quartet, now a trio.
**Musgrave:** short philanderer, no good in a fight.
**Nancy:**
(1): feckless female, cf Polly.
(2): who's a pretty boy then?
(3): type of whiskey.
**Polly:**
(1): woman on shore. Pregnant, short sighted or both. Often has store of money for issue, see Sailors & Fiddle (2).
(2): talkative parrot, easily bribed.
**Robin Hood:** writer of over-long and self-congratulatory ballads.
**Spencer:** a footballer.
**Taylor:** general, deceased and absent.
**William:** sweet, usually absent.

# ◆ TRADITIONAL STEREOTYPES

**Babes:** pretty, usually lost in the wood or abandoned (see Ladies).

**Bailiffs:**
(1): they have daughters.
(2): see Poachers and Australia.

**Beggars:** always pretend to be royalty, see Maidens and Doors.
**Blacksmiths:** they always hold it in their hand.

**Captains:** bewhiskered, can have ice in eye. Often marry "sailors" (see Cross-dressing)
**Chambermaids:** unlike normal Maidens they inevitably get the better of their suitors.

**Gardeners:** often found standing-by, offering flowers to indecisive females.
**Gypsies:** good at attracting married Ladies; musical, they usually form trios or septets.

**Knights:** tend to be outlandish, low intellect, poor swimmers.

**Ladies:** care little for husbands or children, would rather take on numerous gypsies.
**Lords:** forever abandoned by wives and cuckolded by singing travellers.

**Maidens:** predictably wayward (where do they all come from? Where are they now?)
**Millers:** good at grinding (see Apron Strings), sometimes well hung (see Sisters) or dammed.

**Ploughmen:** tend to whistle and sing.
**Poachers:** one is always shot, the rest transported.

**Sailors:** returning wanderers required to test the fidelity of short sighted/forgetful women.
**Sisters:**
(1): either fair & dead, or ugly & vindictive.
(2): silly.
**Squires:** wealthy, young, and untrustworthy.

**Tailors:** the butt of folk jokes. Tend to have domineering and unfaithful wives.
**Tinkers:** see Beggars.

# ◆ FOLK GEOGRAPHY

**Albion:** perfidious and banned.
**Amerikay:** always misspelt. Many go, leaving sweethearts by the dozen. No one ever returns.
**Australia:** destination of hapless poachers. (They're still at it!) and Eric Bogle.

**Cape Horn:** for rounding, shantyman's equivalent of Piccadilly Circus.

**Downs:** place where fleets lie, awaiting the inevitable arrival of boat loads of sweethearts.

**English:**
(1): the bane of the Scots.
(2): the bane of the Irish.
(3): the bane of everyone else.
(4): victorious, regardless of history.

**French:** the enemy, always defeated regardless.
**Greenland:** regular venue for unsuccessful whaling.

**Holland:** see Lowlands.

**Irish:**
(1): the bane of the English.
(2): inventors of folk music.

**Lowlands:** low and away, good for drowning.

**Mexico:** noted for plains and a circular bay.

**Scots:** the bane of the English.
**Spanish:** the other enemy, also prone to defeat.

**Van Diemens Land:** original terminus of the Pentonville shuttle.

## ♦ ICONS IN THE TRADITION

**Apron Strings:** fastenings of variable altitude and length.
**Barley Mow:** always requires good luck (see Pint Pot).
**Barrel:**
(1): variable size, must be set upright.
(2): impromptu garment worn by Tinker.

**Baskets:** full of oysters, butter and bastards.
**Breasts:** lily-white, always inadvertently exposed at sea (see Cross Dressing).

**Breeches:** always worn by rapidly departing
**Chambermaids** (along with watch, purse, etc)

**Cannons:** loud weapons, always roaring.
**Cockades:** of variable colour, always worn by departing males.

**Doors:** essential for kissing maidens behind.
**Drum:** device for rescuing soldiers from possessive females.

**Fife:** see Drum.
**Firkin:** see Barrel, & Apron Strings.

**Gales:** always sweet and pleasant.
**Gallows:** can be danced round, often venue for last song of the evening.
**Guns:** rattling firearms.

**King's Shilling:** see Fife.
**Knot:** posthumous arboreal bowline found in graveyards.

**May:** a month full of mornings.

**Pint Pot:** container in need of good luck.
**Pistols:** always by the brace and at the side.

**Ring:** inevitably split, pieces subsequently rediscovered by short-sighted women.

**Sovereigns:** always bright.
**Spring-time:** when people return.

# ◆ FOLK PASTIMES

**Cross-dressing:** con-trick used by possessive females (see Traditional).

**Eavesdropping:** common storytellers activity.

**Fiddling:** see Knapsacks and Maidens

**Hunting:** no wonder the wildlife of this place is depleted. Our forebears spent days killing it and nights singing about killing it.

**Voyeurism:** another regular storytellers' pastime.

**Watching:** fishes gliding, waters sweetly flowing, lambs sporting and playing, etc. Usually a precursor to Fiddling.

# ◆ FOLK FLORA AND FAUNA

**Briar:** tends to entwine.
**Buffalo:** either plain or hunted.
**Dove:** boring symbol of affection. Relative of **Pigeon** (as in pie)

**Fox:** noble but doomed.
**Geese (farmyard):** not a hope (see Fox).
**Geese (wild):** likewise.
**Hares:** innocent but doomed.
**Hounds:** bloodthirsty dogs with stupid names.
**Ivy:** tends to grow around doors.

**Kangaroo:** clearly watertight.
**Lambs:** forever at sport and play.
**Parrot:** spies on maids late at Knight.
**Rose:** see Briar and Knot.
**Thyme:** comes in bunches, often lost or stolen.
**Turtle:** see Dove

**Whales:** unfortunate animals, noted for upsetting boats and Captains.
**Willow:** always being stripped.
**Woodbine:** see Ivy.

## ◆ FOLK ALEMENTS

**Bent Ear:** see Ladies Morris.
**Broken Ankle:** see Sword dance.
**Broken Head:** see Morris dance.
**Broken Jaw:** see Clog.
**Broken Wrist:** see Rapper or Bodhran.

**Deaf:**
(1): see Folk Rock.
(2): see Finger Stuck In Ear.

**Finger Stuck In Ear:** see Song, Traditional.
**Headache:** see Ambience, Autoharp, Bodhran, Tuning.

**Insomnia:** see Bodhran & Folk Festival.
**PMT:** female ailment observed after Ralph McTell concerts.

**Repetitive Strain Injury:** see Bodhran.
**Roving Eye** (usually dark as well).
**Sleep:** see Ballad.
**Trench Foot:** see Folk Festival.

## ◆ ELECTRONICS FOR FOLKIES

**Amplifier:**
(1) Vital accessory for fibreglass guitars.
(2) Device for deafening dancers at a ceilidh.
(3) One warm enough to do jacket potatoes.

**Balance:**
(1) meaningless concept, the drums and accordion will always be too loud.
(2) what you can't do after too much ambience.
(see Quartet, Bar line, and Scotch Snap).

**Bug:** see Camp Site and Cornflakes.
**Equaliser:** block heels & a lead-lined handbag.

**Feedback:** technique for waking the back row.
**Fold Back:** audio equivalent of the King's New Clothes.

**High Voltage:** energetic dance technique.
(AC/DC is nothing to do with Ladies morris.)
**Loudspeaker**: see MC.